~Purpose Found Me~

"For I know the plans I have for you"

Dr. Tammy Morgan

Copyright © 2019 Dr. Tammy Morgan

All rights reserved.

ISBN: 978-1946106490

DEDICATION

My mom, Rosetta Crowder

No part of this book may be reproduced, or copied without written permission from the author.

Quoted verses of scripture throughout this book are taken from the Holy Bible, King James Version, and the New International Version (NIV).

All scripture quotations are taken from the Authorized King James Version of the Holy Bible, unless otherwise noted.

CONTENTS

Acknowledgments   i

1 Unforgettable Season

2 The Journey

3 Another Interruption

4 The Road to healing

5 Founding My Way Again

6 Are You Ready

7 Here I Go Again

8 Say What Now Lord?

9 My Journey Home

ACKNOWLEDGMENTS

Thank you pastor Lynn Rentz for taking the time out of your busy schedule to edit and proofread pages after pages…love you!

CHAPTER ONE

~My unforgettable Season~

Looking back on my journey I often find myself sharing my experiences by introducing my story, "PURPOSE FOUND ME."

I remember the day that changed my world, as if it was taking place at this very moment….. As I listen to the birds outside my window and the sound of rain hitting against the ground. I can also hear the woodpecker peck at the oak tree near my bedroom window. I glance down at my bible and couldn't help but notice what the highlighted page was turned to. "*Finally my brother rejoice in the Lord."* Paul's choice of words drew my attention. It was as if Paul was writing directly to me; addressing an end to a season, instructing me, and the church to rejoice.

Finally my brother!
HAS MY TIME OF REJOICING COME? OR HAVE I ALLOWED MY "WHEN I WAS" TO DISTRACT ME FROM ALLOWING PURPOSE TO FIND ME?

Up till the age of six, life had appeared to be good, from the eyes of a 6 year old little girl. I was born into a family of prophets, evangelists and pastors, but I was not yet aware of this prophetic lineage. I do not have memories of ever attending church with my mom and dad while living in North Carolina; my birth state.

But I do have fond memories of the large house we lived in, and the huge backyard with a small pond stream behind our house, it was a beautiful neighborhood. Life was good, so I thought.

We had a home of five. My mother and father, my older brother, an older sister, who I never got the opportunity to know, and yes!

ME….the baby girl. I had everything a little girl could have hoped for until tragedy stuck my family, leaving me to be the only daughter, and the last child my mother would birth into this world. The time I shared with my mother was cut short, very short, leaving me only bits and pieces of her memory. I can remember her smile from a distance. But as the year's passed, her smile has faded and I can only see her through a cloudy pair of glasses. I do not remember her touch. I do not remember her voice. I can only remember the warm thoughts of how kind and loving she was to me….*O how I treasure those thoughts of her.*

After the tragic passing of my sister and mother, life went on. However, not the life as I once knew it to be.

CHAPTER TWO

~THE JOURNEY~

My journey has now made a drastic shift. Not aware that God had a plan for me, yes! Even at the age of six, God was working things out for my good. You may not understand where and why your journey has led you to low places, rainy forests and sometimes through dark woods. But understand this! God has a plan for you and he is always with you!

God told Jacob, *"when you pass through the waters I will be with you and when you pass through the rivers they shall not overflow you when you walk through the fire you shall not be burned neither shall the flame kindle upon you."* Isaiah 46:2

When you totally place your trust in God… Purpose will find you! Peace will comfort you!

I don't have a microwave quick fix for you. However, I do know if you submerge your mind with the word of God, and your heart with the love of Christ, whatever season you're in and whatever you are being challenged with you will come out victoriously!

When I was nine, I remember having

my first spiritual vision. Being only nine, I thought it was peculiar. But God chose that time and that place to introduce me to Him, and the spiritual gifts that He had placed in me. The enemy also had a plan; his plan was to use my first experience with God to quiet the voice of the prophet.

I remember my experience as though it was yesterday.

THE VISION

It was a cloudy gray day. It seemed as

if I were standing right there in the midst of it all. It almost felt as if I was in a movie scene. There before me was a huge house like castle and there were many flowers being laid out in front of the gate. Though it was a cloudy gloomy day, I did not feel afraid and I knew I was not alone. I asked why are them laying flowers at the gate? I heard a gentle voice speak these words, "They are preparing for your grandmother." Still I felt no fear. The very next morning I knew something strange just happened. …so I ran to tell my older brother about my experience….. **BUT WAIT! Let me**

back up to a few years prior.

After my mother passed away, everything about my life changed my home, city, state, and even the people in my life; who are now my newly discovered family.

I remember the summer of 1973 so vividly, the day mother boarded me and my brother on the plane heading to Detroit. I've been on planes before because my dad was stationed in many places throughout his Army career, so boarding planes wasn't unfamiliar to me. But this particular day the chain of events went a little differently. As the flight attendant directed my brother and me to our seats, I noticed my mother waving at us from the gate. Being only 6 I did not understand why my mother wasn't boarding the plane with us, but as I think back I'm sure my older brother was given instructions to watch after his baby sister. My brother remained strong as he tried to console me …. You talk about a kid crying on the plane, let me tell you it wasn't pretty… I would have cried all the way to Detroit if it had not been for the pilot who allowed me to visit the cockpit. I often wonder if the dramatic experience of that day was the root cause of my fear of flying.

Though my mother had a successful nursing career and my father a successful military career, home life wasn't what it had appeared to be.

Shortly after our arrival to Detroit I witnessed the horrifying homicide of my mother committed by my father.

Now homeless and parentless my brother and I went from having more than enough to struggling to have just barely enough. I watched how my aunt would stretch her paycheck to care for two additional people, while waiting for our SSI checks to make ends meet.

Though my auntie was a nurse as well and made good wages, we were not a part of her original plan. However, I was grateful that she provided my brother and me a good loving home.

My grandmother was the disciplinarian, and let me tell you, this new way of parenting I had to adapt to very quickly.

For three years my grandmother took on the role of raising my brother and me, until God took her home.

Now as I mentioned prior I ran to share my vision with my brother. I was young and I've never had anything happen like this before to me. So, I shared step-by-step details with my brother of my experience. My brother didn't have much to say about my vision, he just listened.

Shortly after that experience my grandmother passed away. I lived with the idea that I was the cause of this awful thing that had just happened to both my mother and grandmother. I was blamed for many years that I was the cause of my mother's death due to sharing what I thought I witnessed. Again I felt if only I would have just kept my mouth shut about what I saw and about this vision these awful things would not have happened. So of course the enemy used these experiences to quiet my voice. I was afraid to speak what God showed me in visions and afraid to share the supernatural experiences God would allow me to have. Visions of heaven and visions of His coming, how beautiful these visions were. Instead I became shy and withdrawn. Growing up thinking I was the cause of my mother's and grandmother's death. Growing up afraid to speak, and disliking the voice God had given me.

The lies the enemy plants to try to kill your destiny and your purpose. But Jesus came to give you, ***"life and life more abundantly."***

I want to stop here to pray for you,

"Father I break the stronghold over your people and I cancel out Satan's lying spirit assignment to shut the mouths of your prophets, evangelists, pastors and teachers with the fire of the Holy Spirit! Father release Your Glory on your people and release the prophetic anointing on your people! Let your words flow like a river through your people let them be bold and strong in you in Jesus name!   AMEN!

FULLY IN ENGAGED

Though, Satan tried to continue to plant little seeds of corruption in other areas of my life, I continued to overcome by prayer and serving in my church.

Now attending church on a regular basic

I joined the choir at my church, "The Original Church of God." Needless to say I was now being raised in a very strict household. I was not allowed to wear pants, makeup, earrings or any other clothing that did not resemble holiness. I happily helped the spiritual mothers in the kitchen. I visited nursing homes and witnessed with the mothers door to door; that of course was a little bit difficult for me. I was withdrawn inside due to all the terror that had just taken place. Witnessing my dad shoot my mother, my sister getting killed by a drunk driver while she waited for the school bus, and now the passing of my grandmother. Though I served the Lord and went to church on Sunday mornings I still had not yet been introduced to the Holy Spirit and God's healing power of deliverance.

My life was pretty much the same for the next seven years after I arrived in Detroit; until another big interruption changed my life.

Chapter Three

~Another Interruption~

Wow! 2 mothers (*mom and grandmother*) now gone, a dad I thought I would never see again gone, and now another change? Why I thought?

One Sunday morning when I was 13 I was excited about going church. Every Sunday morning I had my routine. I would hurry to get addressed only to watch the first half of my favorite Sunday morning program, "Albert and Costello." But this particular Sunday things were different, I was able to watch the entire episode before heading out to church. As we were driving to church I noticed my aunt had taken a different route. We pulled up in front of this big red brick building. I was wondering where we were as I was looking out the car window.

As we exited the car, I walked hesitantly up the stairway into this red brick building on the hill, it was a church. As I entered the sanctuary my eyes browsed across the room.

I felt the eyes of the other teenagers look toward my brother and me as if to ask, "Who's the new girl?"

As I sat quietly in my seat I observed the preaching style of the preacher. He was full of energy! He was shouting and running across the pulpit. He was nothing like my pastor at my other church, where the only excitement was getting called out by the pastor for talking; and getting the stare down from the church mothers.

Though I didn't know at the time, this new pastor was actually preaching with God's power and anointing. I remember thinking to myself ….these people are crazy!

Finally the service was over. I rushed

down the stairway and ran to the car giving my brother a quick sigh of relief. And then I kept thinking how sad I was that we missed church dinner at our church, and wondering if Mother Smith baked her famous mac and cheese.

We continued to go to this red brick Full Gospel Church on the Hill every single Sunday, never to attend my old church again. I was not ecstatic about leaving the church that became my safe place. A church I grew to love and the people who became my family when I needed them the most.

You're On Your Own This Time

My brother joined the military, so this new church journey I had to take alone.

On Easter Sunday, I realize that God had a plan, and his plan was perfect.

Now attending the new Full Gospel church, finding my place in the back, watching all the people addressed in their Easter best. I remember sitting there in my place refusing to like this church, fighting to like this new pastor's preaching style, but something great was happening to me.

You got my attention

I don't remember the full message on this particular Sunday, but I do remember wanting to hear more. For the first time I was actively listening to what God was saying through the pastor to me. Something within me wanted and needed more of this gospel!

SOMETHING IS HAPPENING

I found myself excited about going to church the following Sunday, but this time I wanted to sit a little closer to the front, so I scanned the room for a closer spot yes! I found a seat in the middle of the church! Not to close, but close enough as to give the message, "I think I like this church, but I still need my personal space."

As I listened to the pastor; who would later become my first spiritual father, the desire to know more of God was bubbling inside me.

I wanted to know more about Jesus. It wasn't just about cooking in the kitchen with the mothers and warming up chocolate donuts for our after Sunday school snack. It wasn't just about singing in the small youth choir anymore or being on the youth usher board. I really wanted to attend church now to learn more about Jesus.

I was excited about Sunday services! I could not wait for Tuesday Bible study. I was excited about Friday night revival services. And now I had new friends who had the same desires that I had. We all desired to seek Christ more!

My friend~ it doesn't matter what age you are, when God gets a hold of you it's the greatest exchange ever! God takes everything the enemy tried to do against you, to you, and gives you the victory over it! Jesus will restore that joy inside of you!!

chapter three text here. Insert chapter three text here.

CHAPTER FOUR
~The Road to Healing~

When I was 14 I received the Holy Spirit! I remember hanging on to every word I heard from the pulpit. The pastor asked, "Who desires to receive the Holy Spirit?" I was so excited that I leaped to my feet. I was running to the front of the line shouting in my spirit "I do! I do!" It was as if no one noticed me as people pushed their way to the front, there I stood in front of my pastor listening to the sound of his voice as he instructed the crowd to just believe.

As he prayed he simply told us to believe. And then he told us to open our mouths to allow the Holy Spirit to speak through us. I started to tremble inside, however I don't think anyone noticed. My body had started feeling like a warming cloth was covering it entirely, and I heard this heavenly voice speak through me…. Wow! I knew God was real at that very moment, just like the pastor had said. I knew I would never forget this beautiful day!

> *"And suddenly there came a sound from heaven as of a rushing mighty wind, and it filled all the house where*

they were sitting. And there appeared unto them cloven tongues like as of fire, and it sat upon each of them. And they were all filled with the Holy Ghost, and began to speak with other tongues, as the Spirit gave them utterance."

Acts 2:2-4

Now being filled with the Holy Spirit the desire for God intensified.

I'm Moving Again!

It was time to move again! But this time I was full of excitement! I'm moving from the middle row, to the 2nd row, away from all the distractions. I knew that God was preparing a special place for me. *"And the Lord said behold there is a place by me and I'll shall stand upon a rock"* Exodus 33:21

And I grew in God.

IS GOD CALLING ME TO MINISTRY?

The dreams and visions I experienced prior did not prepare me for what God was now revealing to me.

Though I experienced dreams and visions prior to my new church, I knew that God was now revealing to me new supernatural experiences. Is God calling me to Ministry?

David was minding his business and doing the things he loved when God interrupted his plans. God had already handpicked David to become King. The great interruption! Hallelujah!

"And Samuel said unto Jesse, Are here all thy children? And he said, There remaineth yet the youngest, and, behold, he keepeth the sheep. And Samuel said unto Jesse, Send and fetch him: for we will not sit down till he come hither. And he sent, and brought him in. Now he was ruddy, and withal

of a beautiful countenance, and goodly to look to. And the LORD said, Arise, anoint him: for this is he."

1 Samuel 16:11-12

I was excited to pray and read my Bible in my prayer closet every day. After being filled with the Holy Spirit, while reading my bible one day in my closet, the Word of God caught my soul on a spiritual revival! I heard the Holy Spirit say, "turn to Acts 2:17" as I read, *"I will pour out of my Spirit upon all flesh: and your sons and daughters shall prophesy"*

I wept at the feet of Jesus in my small little closet on Ohio Street, fourteen years old now and getting trained by God in His school of the prophet. The Holy Spirit led me from scripture to scripture. Before I left my prayer closet I knew without a doubt that God had given me the gift of prophecy and God was putting me on my personal journey to hear and to know His voice.

Confirmation Time

I was excited to get to church the next day; I wanted my pastor to confirm what God was doing in me.
As I stood in the prayer line waiting with high expectations, I realize I didn't have to have a confirmation or

any special prayer prayed over me, I just wanted God's approval. That night I did not get a confirmation or a prayer prayed over me, nor was there a prophecy concerning my purpose. But I felt the heat of the Holy Spirit consume my entire body. This was my first lesson… how to recognize God's voice for myself….

When God calls you to ministry you will receive a personal invitation from HIM first. You will have a personal encounter with HIM. Man does not call you into Ministry.

Understand this, when God calls you,

He will equip you, He will teach and He will send you. When you are relying on man to confirm your call, to confirm your ministry, to confirm your destiny and your purpose… you give man power to control, to delay, to deny, and to disqualify you out of the gifts and the call God has placed in you.

"And Moses said unto God, Behold, when I come unto the children of Israel, and shall say unto them, The God of your fathers hath sent me unto you; and they shall say to me, What is his name? what shall I say unto them?[14] And God said unto Moses, I AM THAT I AM: and he said, Thus shalt thou say unto the

children of Israel, I AM hath sent me unto you." Exodus 3:13-14

I am a true believer of being held accountable and serving another man's ministry, but I don't believe in getting stuck. You have to know God for yourself.

When God sends me to a church, or when I hold revival services, my purpose is to stir up the gifts and calling to bring forth revival to the body of Christ.

CHAPTER FIVE
~FOUNDING MY WAY AGAIN~

As a young teenager I was very engaged in church activities. I attended Mattie Moss Clark concerts and also revival services. But there was another interruption getting ready to happen. I started to hear street rumors regarding the trouble my pastor was in. Because I was young in my walk with Christ, I was fully persuaded that the rumor I was hearing wasn't true.

WHAT JUST HAPPENED?

As we made our way to the church; as we did every Sunday, we discovered upon arrival there would be no church service that particular day. I remember urgently trying to open the church doors. And as I stood in front of the pad locked doors, I cried out to God, asking Him what is happening!! Looking out into the street, hoping that one of the cars passing by would stop and that my pastor would emerge saying, everything is all right and that he was sorry for being late… no cars stopped, my pastor didn't emerge and we didn't have church that day; nor in the months to come.

KEEPING IT REAL

It was only God's love and faithfulness that kept me through this season in my life. The pain, the hurt and the betrayal pierced my heart as I listened to the truth concerning my spiritual father. *"But every man is tempted, when he is drawn away of his own lust, and enticed."* James 1:14

As one of my high school friends; Bishop Brooke's son, revealed the truth to me concerning my pastor, I could no longer turn a deaf ear to what the streets was saying. I had to allow truth to come so God could heal me once again. **But this time the path to healing took a different turn.**

<u>*The Hurting Truth*</u>

After finding out this truth, I turned around from the church. While I prayed and cried out to God, I remember saying these words, "God I love you, but I will never trust another pastor in my life "

Once again I felt lost and abandoned.

But God's Word instructs us to "*Be strong and courageous. Do not be afraid or terrified because of them, for the LORD your God goes with you; he will never leave you nor forsake you."*

I later realized that this level of disappointment was now a deep hurt that opened the door to the enemy. Throughout my years of counseling and teaching others, I've encouraged everyone God has allowed to come into my life to develop a close tight knitted relationship with Jesus. By first knowing who Jesus is through prayer and the studying of God's word, and secondly by knowing who you are in Him. Paul said it best *"For I am persuaded, that neither death, nor life, nor angels, nor principalities, nor powers, nor things present, nor things to come, nor height, nor depth, nor any other creature, shall be able to separate us from the love of God, which is in Christ Jesus our Lord."*

~PURPOSE FOUND ME~

11 year journey.

CHAPTER SIX

~ARE YOU READY~

Now married with my two children, and 9 years later, I was now preparing for a divorce. As I walked down the long hallway toward my waiting attorney, as he reached into his brown leather bag to pull out documents for final review, he gave me a half smile mumbling "Are you ready?" As we entered the courtroom I remembered standing there alone in front of the judge frightened and unsure of my future. After just a few questions it was all over. My dreams, my family, my marriage, over in 3 minutes! No one was there to hold my hand, no one was there encouraging me to be strong. As I left, I shook my attorney's hand holding back my tears to thank him for his service.

The walk down that hallway seemed never-ending as I hurried down the stairs to quickly locate my car to return back to work. I can remember hearing ***"This too shall pass."***

THE RIDE HOME

I felt numb inside, now left alone with two small children and without family support. I remember asking the million-dollar question, now what?

"For I know the plans I have for you, declares the Lord, plans to prosper you and not to harm you, plans to give you hope and a future." **Over and over I heard God say,** *"for I know the plans I have for you."*

YOU SEE T HERE'S NO PREFECT LIFE, BUT GOD HAS A PREFECT PLAN FOR YOUR LIFE

When you feel look life is literally snatching the rug up from under you, remember the battle is not yours. Your battle belongs to the Lord. *"He said: "Listen, King Jehoshaphat and all who live in Judah and Jerusalem! This is what the* L*ORD* *says to you: 'Do not be afraid or discouraged because of this vast army. For the battle is not yours, but God's"* 2 chronicles 20:15

God will defend you, God will protect and He will deliver you out of what might seem to be an impossible situation. *"O my God, I trust in thee: let me not be ashamed, let not mine enemies triumph over me."*
 Psalms 25:2

ALL HE DESIRES FROM YOU IS FOR YOU TO TRUST, LOVE AND OBEY HIM!

"Trust *in the Lord with all thine heart; and lean not unto thine own understanding."* Proverbs 3:5-6

You might be walking through a low valley right now, but believe me when I say, you are NOT alone! The hand of the Lord is guiding you through the valley, His Holy Spirit is with you to comfort you in times of loneliness, and God's power is with you to keep you.

SOMEONE HELP I AM FALLING!

The enemy used all my recent losses and those in my past to detour me from the call that was on my life.

The first two months after my husband left the home took me to a very lonely place; I wanted the hurt to stop so I replaced my healing process with mommy duties, alcohol, and work.

PRAYER NOTES:

CHAPTER SEVEN
~HERE I GO AGAIN~

After work, I would pick up my 1 year old and 7 year old from school and daycare. I would cook and then help my 7 year old son with his homework. We shared a little family time during these evenings before I tucked them safely into their beds…. Fully convinced I wasn't worthy of being loved I tried to hide my pain and depression. But God had different plans for me, as I would soon to find out.

G*ET *UP!

It was time to get myself together. The bible tells us to, *"Shake off your dust; rise up, sit enthroned, Jerusalem. Free yourself from the chains on your neck, Daughter Zion, now a captive."* Isaiah 52:2 *NIV*

I did not have any more tears within me to cry. Wait! Did I finally see stillness at the end of this storm?

"weeping may endure for a night, but joy cometh in the morning. Psalm 30:5

***P*URPOSE IS *C*OMING**

God sent a minister into my life for a

business opportunity, however at the time I had no idea she was a minister.

God will set you up to bring you out!

One day as she was so diligently trying to recruit me to attend one of her business meetings, the Lord opened the opportunity for her to minister to me.

The conversation went something like this:

Minster: hey what are you doing tonight? Do you want to come to our financial planning meeting?

Me: no (very few words)

Minister: it's still early and you can bring your boys with you.

Me: I'm getting ready for bed; and I have work in the morning.

Minister: I've been praying for you and God has shown me you are going through depression. *I recognize it because I was you a few years ago. I went through my divorce and all I wanted to do was sleep through the pain.*

Me: (quiet)

Minister: I'm speaking at my church on Sunday, I would like for you to come.

Me: what time? I'll be there…..

God will send people into your life to

push you back on the path He intends for you to be on. Pushing you back into PURPOSE!

God uncovered the working of the spirit of depression, and He delivered me that night! Placing me back on the path He had already prepared for me!

"whosoever shall call on the name of the LORD shall be delivered: for in mount Zion and in Jerusalem shall be deliverance, as the LORD hath said, and in the remnant whom the LORD shall call." (Joel 2:32)

CHAPTER EIGHT
~SAY WHAT NOW LORD~

I knew God was calling me to minister in the gift of prophecy but never in my wildest dreams did I know God was calling me to teach His people.

After months of many attempts to get me to attend her financial planning meetings, I finally agreed to attend. I'm not sure if the reason why I agreed was based on the desire to learn more about her company, or did I gave in just so she would stop asking, regardless to the reasons why, God used my yes, to get my attention.

Now attending church again, I was ready to meet new people! As soon as I committed to attending her business meeting, I heard the *Holy Spirit* say, **"*you can commit to an hour for someone else but you can't give me 15 minutes to do what I'm calling you to do?*"** I immediately fell to my knees to repent of my disobedience. That very same day I reached out to the local Christian radio station in Detroit to start my first broadcast, Breaking Through to Glory Ministries. I heard the Lord say, *"Eyes hath not seen, nor ear heard, neither have entered into the heart of man, the things which God*

hath prepared for them that love him."
1 Corinthians 2:9

My friend, God is looking for a heart that loves Him. It does not matter what you have done or what was done to you, the Bible tells us, *"to love the Lord your God with all your heart and with all your soul and with all your strength and with all your min*d."
Your yes to Jesus will lead you on a great journey, and as you seek after God your Purpose will find you!

CHAPTER NINE
~MY JOURNEY HOME~

"Brethren, I count not myself to have apprehended: but this one thing I do, forgetting those things which are behind, and reaching forth unto those things which are before, I press toward the mark for the prize of the high calling of God in Christ Jesus." Philippians 3:13-14

God has allowed me to teach healing and deliverance to both men and women throughout this country. I am very humble and grateful that I have been given this purpose.. God has allowed me to learn and study under the leadership of many great men and women. But the leadership of the Holy Spirit has governed my steps and those steps have led me into God's purpose concerning me. If you allow the Holy Spirit to oversee your steps, purpose will find you.

Paul said it best, *"But by the grace of God I am what I am: and his grace which was bestowed upon me was not in vain."*

CHOSEN BY GOD

God did not allow in the beginning for man to confirm my gifts and calling. It was when I gave God my yes and when I started to walk in obedience according to His will concerning my life. Only then did He allow leaders to speak into my life.

Many people are led only by prophecy, but when you are led by the Holy Spirit, prophecy will follow you, and prophecy will confirm what God is doing in your life. God will set you in a place, as He did for Moses to allow you to have an experience with Him.

As you reach a level of maturity in your walk it will lead you on a road of humility, consecration, trust, obedience and purpose.

I want to encourage you to keep your eyes on the Prize.

Start where you are and seek God for a relationship with Him. Allow him to lead you through the valleys, unfamiliar places and the low seasons. . When you feel like you are drowning in the cares of life, I want you to remember Jeremiah 29:11, *"For I know the thoughts that I think toward you, says the Lord, thoughts of peace and not of evil, to give you a future and a hope."*

I prophesy to your spirit! Get up and Come out from your sleep!
Walk in the plan of God concerning

you. Allow God's purpose for you to find you!

Prayer Notes:

Prayer Notes:

Recommendations

"I have known Apostle Tammy since 2014. We met through a mutual friend and what I consider a divine appointment from the Lord. I began Apostle Tammy's School of Ministry in February of 2014. I can tell you, it truly blessed me in directing me to my position in the fivefold ministry, but also seasoned me in my personal walk with Christ. And it was through this divine appointment that I got to know her as a person. Apostle Tammy definitely qualifies in areas of leadership and spirit filled ministry. Before every class began, she was highly sensitive as to set the temperature for the environment spiritually, and to "clear" the airwaves with strong prayer.

One of the most important things that I noticed about her sensitivity to the Holy Spirit was allowing Him to lead the class by His flow and also to end the class time by His flow. One particular student would always have more questions after every teaching, and yet no matter what the time was, Apostle Tammy would take the time to answer. Which shows me how she was concerned more about our needs instead of hers.

She is knowledgeable in the gifts of the Holy Spirit and the purpose of the fivefold ministry. She was deep in the fact of making sure that you understood everything that she taught you. Outside of her being an Apostle, Tammy Morgan is a very awesome and spirit filled woman of God. Her love for Yahweh, Jesus and the Holy Spirit is evident in her conversations and any kind of media.

She is a caring individual and continues to be responsible for assignments that the Lord has given to her. If I need prayer or any kind of help, I know that I could go to Apostle Tammy because she has shown this side of her character to me.

I have been blessed to have been ordained by her. Blessed to have had a season of being taught by her. And now blessed to call her a friend and sister in Christ. Grateful to our Lord to know her."

Pastor Lynn M. Rentz

Recommendations

"I have known Dr. Tammy Morgan for 10 years. She has a great dedication and devotion to the work which God has called her to do. She has a tireless work ethic and has a positive attitude to the people of God. She has shown herself to be honorable, steadfast, and obedient to all that God has called her to accomplish. Apostle Tammy is a strong leader. She is always available to help those in need and she offers great spiritual advice and direction as God leads her. She has a great ability to handle business matters quickly and effectively. I have been very blessed to know this Great Woman of God.

Pastor Peggy Brandon

"Apostle Tammy Morgan is a dedicated person concerning the gospel of Jesus Christ. I have known her for over 10 years and it is an honor to write this letter of recommendation. She has always strived to carry the word of the Lord where ever she sets her feet. She is a great ambassador of Jesus Christ. She is motivated and has a heart to carry the word of the gospel. I have known her to hold revivals for the growth and to revive the

kingdom of God in believers as well as nonbelievers.

In these years of knowing her; she has exhorted, encouraged, and prayed for those who are hurting and crying out for deliverance. I love her humble spirit and cherish her love for the gospel of Jesus Christ."

Prophet Carolyn Thomas-Cain

ABOUT THE AUTHOR

Dr. Tammy Morgan was born in Fayetteville North Carolina. Tammy is the founder and CEO of Breakthrough to Glory Ministries established November 12, 1997. Breakthrough to Glory "Walking in Victory" radio ministry aired for the first time in Detroit Michigan, and later in Texas, GA, Tennessee, Florida, Massachusetts and some parts of Africa. Dr. Tammy travels teaching and equipping the body of Christ to walk in their purpose and destiny.

2006 Tammy founded G.I.V.E women mentorship program for young unwed mothers in whom she mentored young mothers through the COTS homeless shelter program, Peggy's House located in Detroit Michigan, and while in Phoenix Arizona she introduced G.I.V.E mentorship work program at "St. Joseph The Worker " work program in which she was able to employ women transitioning back into the workplace.

Dr. Tammy has a unique and peculiar anointing that brings restoration, healing, and deliverance to the body of Christ. Dr. Tammy has traveled with the mothers of Zion since the age of 6, with prayer being the foundation of her ministry. Tammy was ordained and affirmed into the offices of an Apostle, Prophet, Evangelist, Pastor and Teacher in 2013. She serves as an EPIC prayer leader at EPIC Global Network under the leadership of Apostle Axel Sippach.

Dr. Tammy Morgan has a heart and passion for children who struggles with the tragic loss of one or both parent/parents. In 2017, Dr. Tammy founded "Rosetta's Children Foundation." Rosetta's Children Foundation focuses on providing referrals in counseling for grieving children. Tammy's passion is to please God through her acts of obedience to His Word, and through acts of charity. God has opened many doors for Dr. Tammy to serve her community and He has used her over the years to minister healing through the healing power of the Holy Spirit. In 2014, the School of Ministry was established to train, and to equip the Five Fold Ministry to going out into the vineyard.

2019 Dr, Tammy received her Honorary Doctorate of Divinity and Humanities from Heart Bible Institute University.

www.ingramcontent.com/pod-product-compliance
Lightning Source LLC
Chambersburg PA
CBHW060348050426
42449CB00011B/2878